DOG THERAPY

The Book of Happiness

ACKNOWLEDGEMENTS

Thank you to all our furry participants!

Abby, Bella, Bentley, Bob, Breeze, Cassy, Chewie, Coco, Elsa, Fletcher, Frankie, Indy, Hughey, Jesse, June, Kona, Lily, Lola, Mischa, Pogo, Ralphie, Rza, Sadie (we miss you girl), Sammy, Scamp, Stella, Stella, Timber, Tucker, Wiley.

Off leash hiking dogs are wearing GPS collars for tracking purposes.

Copyright © 2020 by Katy Wilson

FIRST EDITION

This book is dedicated to Pogo, my sidekick and soulmate for eight years. After being diagnosed with a brain tumor and given a year to live, she is still going strong three years later. I am grateful for every extra second I have her by my side.

In memory of our friend Yumi - dog mom to Mischa and avid animal lover, 50 cents* from every book sold will be donated to S.A.I.N.T.S rescue, a sanctuary for senior and special needs animals who have nowhere else to go.
For more information go to www.saintsrescue.ca
*or currency equivalent in country of sale

ACCEPTANCE

Acceptance is not resignation.

Having acceptance doesn't mean we don't want
our situation to be different. It means right now,
in this second, I acknowledge this is difficult
and I feel sad/angry/disappointed.

Find the freedom in acceptance.
Pain cannot be avoided but suffering can.

ANGER

Anger isn't always a problem, in fact it has good intentions. The problem can occur in how we express it.

Be curious about your anger.

Is it pushing people away to keep you safe? Or perhaps it's giving you the drive and energy to stand up against something that is wrong.

Ask what feeling is underneath the anger, because anger is rarely on its own.

ANXIETY

The more we feed the anxiety monster the hungrier it gets. Next time it shows up tell your anxiety that you notice it, you appreciate it trying to keep you safe, and you are going to get through the discomfort anyway.

Picture your anxiety as a cute monster, one that has good intentions but is trying too hard to keep you safe. Have compassion for your anxiety instead of rejecting it.

Pushing feelings away only makes them stronger.

BUILDING POSITIVITY

Our brains are negatively biased. This is not just to be difficult, this is for our survival.

Our brain doesn't scan the world looking for signs of fun. It's looking for danger, for harm, for threats to our wellbeing.

We have to orient our brains to the good stuff ourselves. Pay attention to positive mental experiences.

Train your brain!

CALMING

In moments of emotional intensity and stress, try tensing and then releasing your muscles in different parts of your body.

Start by tensing your fist, taking care not to tense so hard that you cause a strain. Hold for five seconds and notice how it feels, then quickly release and really tune in to that sensation of letting go.

Keep going through all your muscles, if you prefer you can start at your feet and work all the way up!

CONTROL

Do you find yourself needing to be in control?

Controlling aspects of our environment might help us feel safe, but it doesn't help us heal.

Perhaps in the past something negative has happened that wasn't part of "the plan" so your threat detecting brain is trying to do whatever it can to avoid any surprises.

Pay attention to when your controlling part is activated. Notice it, smile, and maybe even have a dialogue with it - let it know you're aware of what's happening and why.

Start to feel the freedom of not needing to control everything to feel safe.

EXPRESSING NEEDS

Have you ever felt disappointed, rejected or misunderstood because someone didn't respond to your obvious sadness, distress or anger? You're not alone!

Due to the illusion of transparency, a cognitive bias, we often wrongly assume that people around us know what we are feeling and therefore know what we need.

They often don't. We need to tell them.

We are simply not as transparent as we think.

GENTLENESS

Five minutes of mindfulness is more helpful
than "I should have meditated."

A walk around the block is more helpful than
"I should have gone to the gym."

"I did the best I can today" is more helpful than
"I should have done better."

Celebrate what you do achieve today, rather
than feel guilt for what you don't.

GRATITUDE

Gratitude brings with it so many mental health benefits. Start by writing down three things every day that you are grateful for, however small.

Alternatively, keep a gratitude jar, add to it on the days you can connect with gratitude and take from it on the days you struggle.

Gratitude can provide contentment, can strengthen relationships, and it costs nothing!

GROUNDING

When you experience challenging emotions, or you feel triggered by a situation, try a grounding exercise with your senses.

Sight: what can you see around you?

Sound: what can you hear? Separate the sounds.

Touch: what can you feel touching your skin?

Smell: what can you smell in the air?

Taste: what can you taste?

Focus on just one sense or try all five - whatever works best for you.

HEALING

When you notice you are reacting to something with intense or overwhelming emotions, ask yourself: "How old is that part of me that is reacting?"

Instead of negatively judging those emotional reactions, have compassion and understanding that the reaction might be from a younger, scared and hurt part of you that has been triggered by something in the present.

INNER CHILD

Your inner child is the you that existed before
the world taught you not to be yourself.

Take time to connect with your inner child.
They are still inside you and need
your attention.

Try writing with your non-dominant hand, or
eating messy food with your fingers, make
animal noises, pull faces in the mirror - have
fun with yourself!

Allow your younger self to shine through.

OPENNESS

Uncomfortable feelings are less uncomfortable when they are permitted.

Instead of playing a constant and exhausting game of whack-a-mole with uncomfortable emotions, try letting the "mole" be there, acknowledge it and allow some space for it. Allow for the possibility that the distress you feel is in the battle against the emotion, rather than the emotion itself.

Today, try letting those unpleasant or uncomfortable feelings be present, acknowledge them, say hi to them just let them be.

Notice what happens for you.

POSITIVE LANGUAGE

We, as humans, have a tendency to judge
ourselves harshly.

In evaluating your life and aspects you might
want to change, think less in terms of good and
bad, healthy and unhealthy,
normal and abnormal.

Think more in terms of helpful and unhelpful.

Language matters. Be gentle.

REGULATION

Our brain acts like a smoke alarm; it wants to
keep us safe and sometimes it makes a lot of
noise even when there isn't a fire.

When that noise is happening we are blocked
from accessing our prefrontal cortex (rational
brain) until our system is regulated enough.

Breathing, visualization, music, and touch are
all ways of self soothing.

Take time to explore ways that work for you.

RELATIONSHIPS

When we are having an emotionally
challenging conversation, allowing for a
little bit of space before we respond gives us a
chance to check our filter. This means we can
check in on what we might be bringing to the
interpretation of what's being said.

Other people have filters too, so remember their
reactions may be coming from months or even
many years ago and have little or nothing to do
with you and the situation you are in.

RELAXATION

Describe in-depth what would be your perfect
place to be. Imagine it in detail, whereabouts
would you be? Who would be with you?
A person? An animal?

What would you eat? What would you hear?
What would you be seeing?
What would you feel?

Immerse yourself in the experience and notice
how your body reacts.

Remember it is somewhere you can take
yourself back to.

SELF-BELIEF

But what if you could?

Self-doubt and our inner critic have an amazing ability to crush our confidence in ourselves.

Instead of listening to your inner voice trying to convince you that you aren't good enough or capable enough, ask yourself:

But what if I could?

SELF-COMPASSION

To foster self-compassion, try to imagine how you would react to a good friend going through whatever you're going through.

What would you say? How would you show them you care? See if you can do the same for yourself.

Perhaps write to yourself from the perspective of that friend. A friend who is accepting, kind, unconditionally loving, and without judgment.

SELF-LOVE

If there was a small child in front of you, who
was scared and upset and you were the only
person there, how would you comfort them?

If they didn't listen to you would you
walk away or try again?

Remember that child is you.

SELF-WORTH

Though you can't yet feel that you are a survivor, worthy of care, strong, brave and inspiring, know that your pet already sees you this way.

STRESS

Our window of tolerance is a zone in which we can go through our day effectively, dealing with challenges, coping with imperfections and still being OK.

When we are outside our window of tolerance, often during times of stress, tiredness, or pain, we can find ourselves becoming more easily overwhelmed.

By being aware and checking in on your own window of tolerance you can tell if it might be time to take a break for some self-care, or perhaps express to someone close to you that you are in need of some support or space today.

TRUE-SELF

Remember what you were like before you were
aware of the eyes of the world making
judgments upon you.

How did you laugh? How did you let go?
How did you express yourself?
What did you hope for?

It's still there inside you.

VALUES

Our values help us to navigate and evaluate our way of being in the world.

These aren't goals, they are principles by which we want to live our lives and interact with other people.

Write down the values you have in life.

Note the qualities that are important to you.

Every day notice if your actions and words are in line with your values.

VULNERABILITY

Today when someone asks you how you are,
instead of saying: "I'm fine," tell them how you
feel. This helps you and it also helps them for
when they need to let people know
they aren't OK.

By keeping others in the dark,
we keep ourselves there too.

WE ARE ONE

Recent world events are like a permanently smoldering fire for our brain's threat detection system.

Our protective parts are activated.

Our windows of tolerance are a little smaller.

Take a minute.

Take a breath.

You are doing really well.

You are not alone. Reach out.